Introduction to Salesforce for Sales
(SPSA-101)

Authors: Dana Cowden, Steve Wasula

1

Notes

1

Agenda

- **Welcome & Introductions**
- Setting up a Practice Site
- Terminology
- A Tour of Salesforce
- Leads
- Activities
- Converting Leads
- Accounts
- Contacts
- Opportunities
- Reports & Dashboards
- Putting it All Together
- Cool Tips!

2

Notes

2

What's In It For Me?

An Easy to Use and Convenient Tool

- A single place to build and manage your business

A Clear View of My Data

- Chatter
- Leads
- Accounts
- Contacts
- Opportunities
- Activity management – Call Reports & Events

More Organized

- Manage activities and track results
- All Account Information is available in one screen

Simple to Make and Read Reporting & Analytics

- Real time and on-demand reporting
- Quickly Run Reports and Dashboards (graphs)

3

Notes

3

Overview

- About this Course
- About the Instructor
- Course Structure
  - Scenario
  - High Level Steps
  - Screenshots/Demo within Application by Instructor
  - Step/Action (Hands-on Exercise)
- Course Materials

4

Notes

4

Agenda

- ▶ Welcome & Introductions
- ▶ **Setting up a Practice Site**
- ▶ Terminology
- ▶ A Tour of Salesforce
- ▶ Leads
- ▶ Activities
- ▶ Converting Leads
- ▶ Accounts
- ▶ Contacts
- ▶ Opportunities
- ▶ Reports & Dashboards
- ▶ Putting it All Together
- ▶ Cool Tips!

5

Notes

  5

Your Practice Site

STONYPOINT

For this hands-on training class, you will need to set up a **Salesforce Developer Edition** to perform the class exercises.

The **Salesforce Developer Edition** is a completely free testing environment that contains a minimal amount of test data and will be available to you forever.

Perform the following steps to set up a Developer Edition for hands-on exercises in this class.

6

Notes

6

Practice Site Action Steps

1. Go to http://developer.force.com
2. Click on the link "Get a Free Developer Edition"

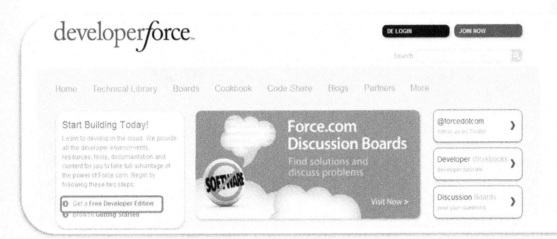

7

Notes

Practice Site Action Steps

3. Fill out the form provided to set up your developer's edition and click *Submit*

   *Username Format: youremailaddress.dev
   (sarah@acme.com.dev)

Get Started Developing on the Force.com Platform

Fill out the fields below and accept our terms of use. You'll receive an email with credentials to your free Developer Edition environment, which also allows you to participate in community forums such as the Discussion Boards, previews and webinars, as well as receive benefits such as the newsletter.

About You

First Name:*

Last Name:*

Email Address:*

Primary Job Role:*   Choose one…

Your Location

Country:*   United States

State/Province:*

Postal Code:*

Developer Force Username

Select a unique username in the form of an email by which you will access your Developer Edition account.

Username *

For Your Security

dodkase Ørsted,

Type the two words:

☐ I have read and agreed to the Master Subscription Agreement

[Submit]

8

Notes

8

Practice Site Action Steps

4. Check your email inbox associated with your developer edition

5. Click on the link within the email from Salesforce to login to your developer edition

```
Welcome to Force.com Developer Edition.
Dear Dana Cowden,

Your user name is below. Note that it is in the form of an email address:

User name: dana@training.com.dev

You'll be asked to set a password and password question and answer when you first log in.
Passwords are case sensitive.
Your password question and answer will be used if you forget your password. Make sure to choose a password question and
answer that you will easily remember.

Click https://login.salesforce.com?c=l14m45n2Bp8yq4eYXCM2L7Ej5R3swJzRTgaSIfMZadIgiptjd6.jSLjh1GhOugvI4I5JRbmKRImg%3D%3D to
log in now.
```

9

Notes

Practice Site Action Steps

6. Create your new password and security question
7. Click **Save** to log in to your new developer edition

10

Notes

Activities Tab Plus

You will also need to install the Activities Tab Plus for use in this class.

The Activities Tab Plus is a tool that allows you to better manage your activities within Salesforce.

Perform the following steps to install the Activities Tab Plus.

*Activities Tab Plus is a completely free app that must be installed by an administrator in your company's instance of Salesforce.

11

Notes

11

Installing Activities Tab Plus Action Steps

1. Login to your developer edition of salesforce.com
2. Click on the force.com app menu in the upper right hand of the home page
3. Select *Add AppExchange Apps...*

12

Notes

4. In the Search box, type in *Activities Tab Plus* and hit your **Enter** key

5. Click on the link to access the Activities Tab Plus

13

Notes

6. Click on the *Get It Now* button
7. Select the prompts as shown below and click *Continue*

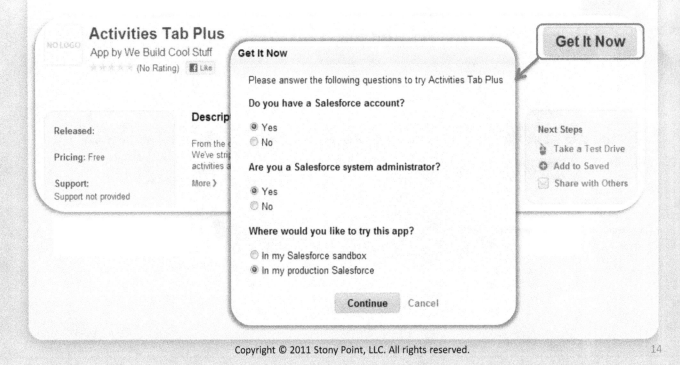

14

Notes

8. Enter your developer edition login credentials
9. Click the *Login* button

15

Notes

Installing Activities Tab Plus Action Steps

10. Check the checkbox to indicate you've read and agree to the terms and conditions
11. Click the **Install** button
12. Enter your password once more and click the **Submit** button

Notes

13. On the Package Installation Details step, click on the **Continue** button

14. In the Application Package API Access step, Click the **Next** button

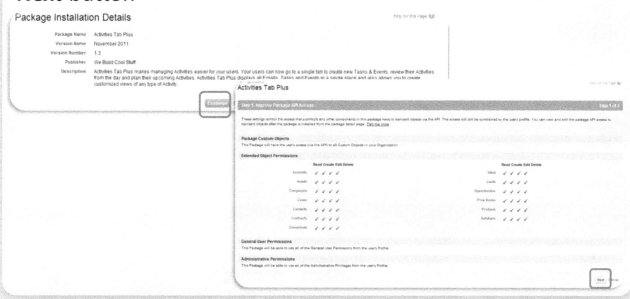

Notes

Installing Activities Tab Plus Action Steps

15. In the Choose Security Model step, select the option *Grant Access to All Users* and click the **Next** button

16. In the final Install Package step, click the **Install** button

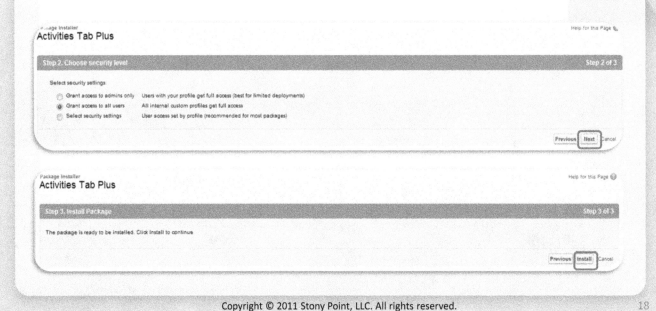

18

Notes

Agenda

▶ Welcome & Introductions
▶ Setting up a Practice Site
▶ **Terminology**
▶ A Tour of Salesforce
▶ Leads
▶ Activities
▶ Converting Leads
▶ Accounts
▶ Contacts
▶ Opportunities
▶ Reports & Dashboards
▶ Putting it All Together
▶ Cool Tips!

Notes

19

Terminology Review

Lead

An unqualified prospect from:
- ❖ Company Website
- ❖ A Call Inquiry
- ❖ A Tradeshow

Opportunity A chance to generate revenue.
- ❖ Acme LLC – 200 Widgets

Account
An organization of any type.
- ❖ Customers
- ❖ Prospects
- ❖ Competitors
- ❖ Vendors

Contact
A person normally associated to an account.
- ❖ CEO
- ❖ Marketing Manager

Report

A real-time detailed list of your business – allowing comparison, tracking, and planning.

Notes

Relationships

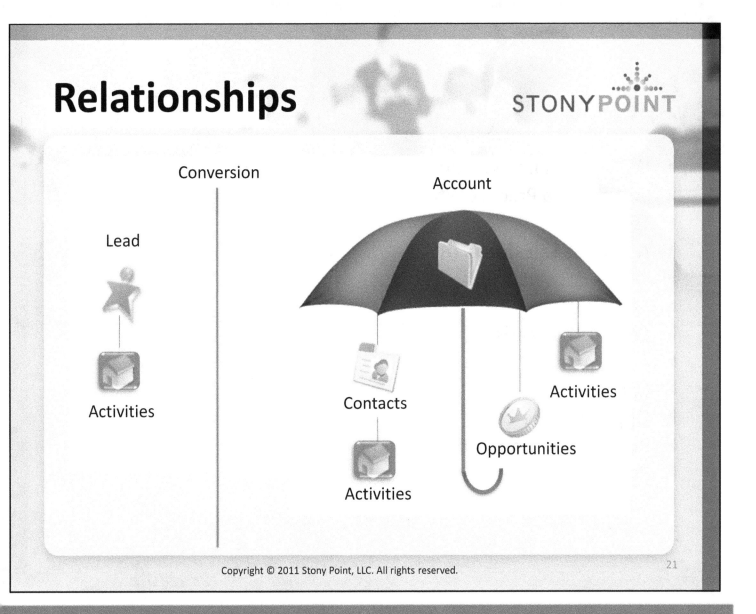

21

Notes

21

Agenda

- ▶ Welcome & Introductions
- ▶ Setting up a Practice Site
- ▶ Terminology
- ▶ **A Tour of Salesforce**
- ▶ Leads
- ▶ Activities
- ▶ Converting Leads
- ▶ Accounts
- ▶ Contacts
- ▶ Opportunities
- ▶ Reports & Dashboards
- ▶ Putting it All Together
- ▶ Cool Tips!

22

Notes

22

Home Page & Navigation

- Your Salesforce.com home page allows you to access a variety of information

Notes

Searching in Salesforce

As a new user of Salesforce, you want to view information on one of your high value accounts in the system, Burlington Textiles.

Use the global search to see the various records stored in Salesforce that are related to Burlington Textiles.

Notes

24

Scenario: Searching for Records

- In the Search Box, enter the name of the Account
- Review the Search Results page to locate any records related to your search
- Click on the name of a record to access it

25

Notes

Searching Tips and Tricks

- Searching is NOT case sensitive
- You must have at least two characters to complete a search
- You have the ability to search using a wildcard (*)
- The search results are grouped by type of record
- Each link within the search results page will take you to a different type of record

Notes

Action Steps: Searching in Salesforce

Goal:

One of the high value customers you work with often is Grand Hotels & Resorts Ltd. You want to locate information stored in Salesforce that is related to the Grand Hotels Account.

Steps:

1. In the search box enter **Grand Hotels**
2. Click the **Search** button
3. Review the search results page
    -   One account and several opportunities should appear
    -   To access the Account, click on the link of the Account Name: **Grand Hotels & Resorts Ltd.**
    -   To access an Opportunity, click on the link of the Opportunity Name: **Grand Hotels SLA**

27

Notes

27

Agenda

- ▶ Welcome & Introductions
- ▶ Setting up a Practice Site
- ▶ Terminology
- ▶ A Tour of Salesforce
- ▶ **Leads**
- ▶ Activities
- ▶ Converting Leads
- ▶ Accounts
- ▶ Contacts
- ▶ Opportunities
- ▶ Reports & Dashboards
- ▶ Putting it All Together
- ▶ Cool Tips!

Notes

Lead Overview

- Think of a Lead as a business card. You have a name and contact information about a person and all you need to do is call them and start the qualification process.

John Smith
ABC Labs

750 N. Orleans
Chicago, IL 60660
jsmith@abc.com

Notes

29

Viewing Leads

STONYPOINT

Leads in Salesforce may have been created by others or come from your website and been assigned to you.

You want to view a list of your unread Leads in Salesforce.

What do you do?

Notes

Scenario: Viewing Your Leads

- Go to the Leads tab
- Select the My Unread Leads View
- Click the *Go!* button

Notes

Action Steps: Viewing Unread Leads

 STONYPOINT

Goal:

You want to view a complete list of your unread Leads in Salesforce. You also need to update the first record within the list to indicate that person has been contacted.

Steps:

1. Click on the Leads tab
2. Select a View
   - My Unread Leads
3. Click the *Go!* button
4. Review the Lead records in your list
   - Click on the name of a Lead to access the record and view the details
5. Click the *Edit* button to update the Lead details
   - Update Lead status to Contacted

Notes

32

Creating a New Lead

You receive a call from John Smith at ABC Labs. He is interested in your company's products or services.

What do you do?

Notes

33

Scenario: Creating a Lead

- Search for John Smith in Salesforce.com
  - Avoid duplicates
- Enter John Smith as a new lead in Salesforce.com
- Save the lead record

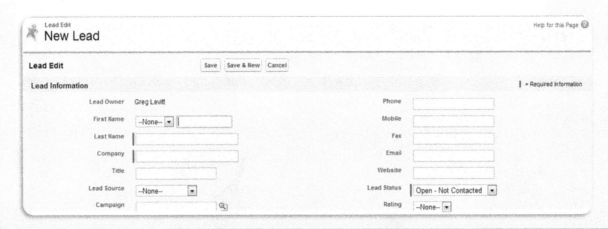

34

Notes

34

Action Steps: Creating a New Lead

Goal:

You receive a call from Lauren Wilson with Stony International. You need to create a new Lead record for Lauren Wilson in Salesforce.

Steps:

1. Search for the last name *Wilson* in the search box
2. Access the Leads tab, and click the **New** button
3. Enter Lauren Wilson's information:

   Name: Lauren Wilson
   Company: Stony International
   Phone Number: 505.555.5555
   Email Address: lauren@mailinator.com
   Lead Status: Contacted

4. Click the **Save** button

Notes

Agenda

- ▶ Welcome & Introductions
- ▶ Setting up a Practice Site
- ▶ Terminology
- ▶ A Tour of Salesforce
- ▶ Leads
- ▶ **Activities**
- ▶ Converting Leads
- ▶ Accounts
- ▶ Contacts
- ▶ Opportunities
- ▶ Reports & Dashboards
- ▶ Putting it All Together
- ▶ Cool Tips!

Notes

Activities Overview

With Activities you can track key interactions with your customers and prospects. There are different types of activities:

- **Task -** a task is a to-do and will remind you of items to complete. Tasks are assigned a due date. This is your "To Do List".

- **Event -** an event is a date/time sensitive activity with a duration, similar to a calendar appointment.

Notes

Logging a Call & Creating a Task

After creating John Smith as a new lead in Salesforce, you should log the activity on his record and create a reminder for yourself to follow up with him.

What do you do?

Notes

38

Scenario: Log a Call & Create a Task

- Locate John Smith's Lead record in Salesforce
- Log a call from the Activity History related list
- Create a follow up task from the call log screen
- Save the activity record

39

Notes

39

Action Steps: Log a Call & Create a Task

Goal:

Lauren Wilson mentioned that her company Stony International is looking to purchase within two months. Locate Lauren Wilson's Lead record and log your activity from the Activity History related list.

Steps:

1. In your Recent Items list, click on the link for the name **Lauren Wilson**

2. Scroll to the Activity History related list on Lauren's Lead Record and click the **Log a Call** button

3. Enter the following information:
   Subject: Initial point of contact call
   Type: Call
   Comments/Description: Spoke with Lauren on the phone. Stony International is interested in purchasing within the next two months.

4. Click the **Save** button

Notes

Creating an Event

John Smith wants to meet with you this Friday to discuss the product(s) or services his company is interested in.

You want to update your calendar to reflect the meeting date and time.

What do you do?

Notes

Scenario: Creating an Event

- Search for the Lead record
- Create a new Event
- Enter meeting details
- Save the Event record

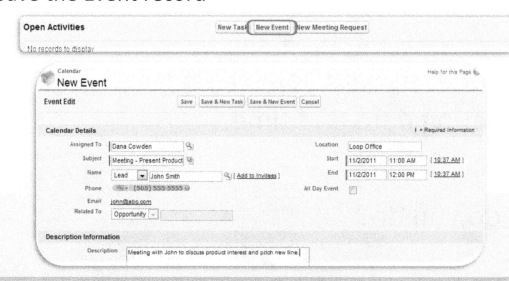

42

Notes

Action Steps: Create a New Event

Goal:

You want to set up an appointment on your calendar to meet with Lauren Wilson and pitch the appropriate products/services that will meet the needs of Stony International.

Steps:

1. Locate and access Lauren Wilson's Lead record
2. Scroll to the Open Activities related list and click the **New Event** button
3. Enter the information:
   Subject: Meeting – Pitch new products
   Location: Loop Office
   Start: Today, 3pm
   End: Today, 4pm
   Description: Meeting with Lauren to pitch new product line.
4. Click the **Save** button

43

Notes

43

Viewing Activities

To view all activities you've created (tasks and events), follow the steps to view the Activities Tab Plus, installed at the beginning of this course.

1. From the home page, select the "+" tab

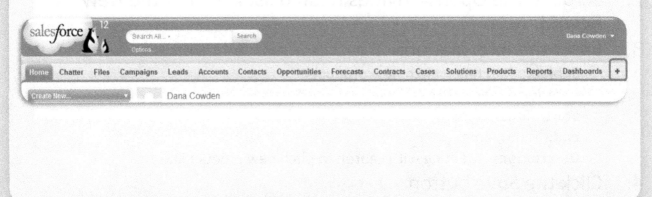

Notes

Viewing Activities

2. Click on the Customize My Tabs button

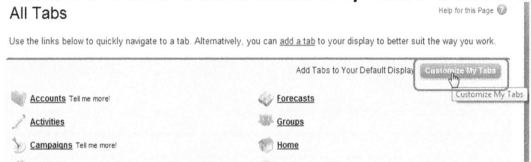

3. Add the Activities Tab

4. Click Save

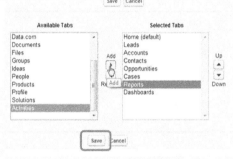

Notes

Viewing Activities

5. Click on the *Activities* tab

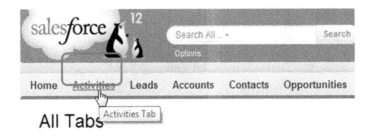

6. Select the *My Activities* view

Notes

Agenda

- ▶ Welcome & Introductions
- ▶ Setting up a Practice Site
- ▶ Terminology
- ▶ A Tour of Salesforce
- ▶ Leads
- ▶ Activities
- ▶ **Converting Leads**
- ▶ Accounts
- ▶ Contacts
- ▶ Opportunities
- ▶ Reports & Dashboards
- ▶ Putting it All Together
- ▶ Cool Tips!

Notes

47

Converting a Lead

After meeting with John, you learn that he has a definite interest in purchasing your company's products/services within the next month and wants to move forward.

Once you've qualified a Lead and feel that you have a viable opportunity with a chance to gain revenue, it is time to convert the Lead into an Account, Contact, and Opportunity.

What should you do?

48

Notes

48

What happens to my converted Lead?

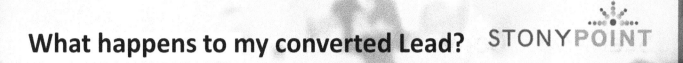

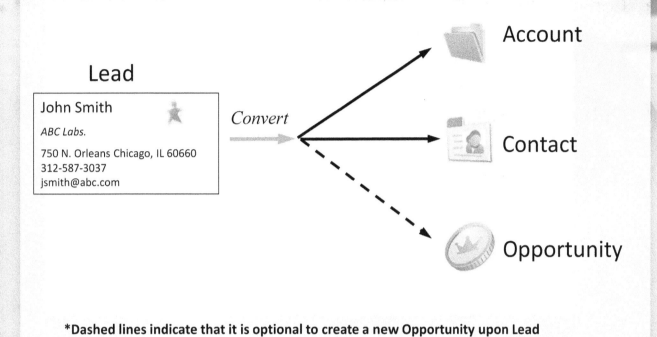

Lead

John Smith
ABC Labs.
750 N. Orleans Chicago, IL 60660
312-587-3037
jsmith@abc.com

Convert

Account

Contact

Opportunity

*Dashed lines indicate that it is optional to create a new Opportunity upon Lead conversion.

49

Notes

49

Scenario: Converting a Lead

- Convert the Lead

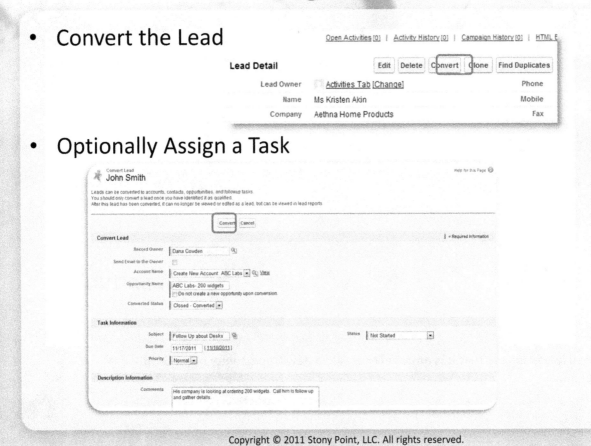

- Optionally Assign a Task

Notes

50

Action Steps: Converting a Lead

Goal:
After speaking with Lauren Wilson regarding her company's interest in purchasing widgets from your company, you've gathered enough information to consider her a qualified Lead. At this point, you need to convert Lauren into an Account, Contact, and Opportunity to begin tracking the revenue in your pipeline.

Steps:
1. Locate and Access Lauren Wilson's Lead Record
2. Click the **Convert** button on Lauren's Lead record
3. Select **Create New Account: Stony International** from the Account Name picklist menu
4. Name the Opportunity:
   Stony International: 200 Widgets
5. Enter the following information to create a task:
   Subject: Follow Up Call for Widget Order
   Due Date: Tomorrow
   Priority: High
   Status: Not Started
   Comments: Stony International wants to order approximately 200 widgets. Call to get more details on time frame.
6. Click the **Convert** button

Notes

Agenda

- ▶ Welcome & Introductions
- ▶ Setting up a Practice Site
- ▶ Terminology
- ▶ A Tour of Salesforce
- ▶ Leads
- ▶ Activities
- ▶ Converting Leads
- ▶ **Accounts**
- ▶ Contacts
- ▶ Opportunities
- ▶ Reports & Dashboards
- ▶ Putting it All Together
- ▶ Cool Tips!

Notes

Account Information

An account can be a company, organization, or business in Salesforce. Accounts provide you with a 30,000 ft view of a company and all records related to that Account.

What Can You See on an Account?

- Strategic account information
- Contacts associated to the account
- Open and historical activities (tasks and events)
- Opportunities

A best practice is to ensure that the Account name is the full legal name of the company/organization.

53

Notes

53

Account Information

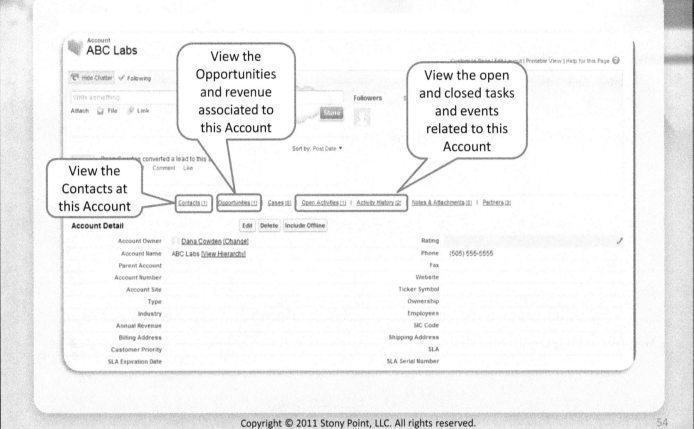

View the Opportunities and revenue associated to this Account

View the open and closed tasks and events related to this Account

View the Contacts at this Account

54

Notes

54

Viewing Account Information

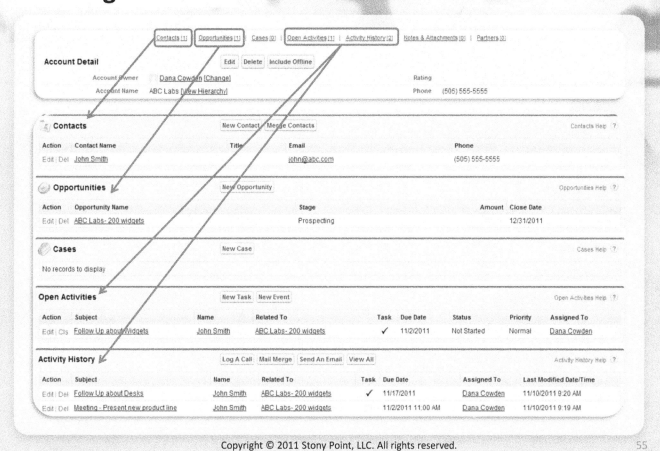

Notes

Agenda

- ▶ Welcome & Introductions
- ▶ Setting up a Practice Site
- ▶ Terminology
- ▶ A Tour of Salesforce
- ▶ Leads
- ▶ Activities
- ▶ Converting Leads
- ▶ Accounts
- ▶ **Contacts**
- ▶ Opportunities
- ▶ Reports & Dashboards
- ▶ Putting it All Together
- ▶ Cool Tips!

Notes

Creating a Contact

You've just received word that Jack Rogers, the main contact at one of your major Accounts, Burlington Textiles, has left the company.

You learn that Sarah Graham will be your new point of contact and work to get her contact information.

What do you do?

Notes

57

Scenario: Creating a Contact

- Search for the correct Account for your new Contact
- From the Account record, create the Contact Record
- Enter Your Contact details and information
- Save your contact record

58

Notes

58

Action Steps: Creating a Contact

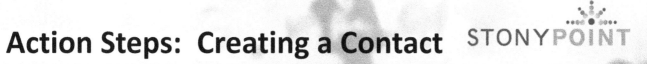
STONYPOINT

Goal:

One of your long time customers Pat Stumuller from Pyramid Construction calls to tell you that she will no longer be working there after next week. She gives you the information for her replacement, Gregory Levitt, who you'll be working with moving forward. Create a new Contact record for Gregory Levitt under the Pyramid Construction, Inc. Account.

Steps:

1. In the global search box, enter the word *Pyramid* and click the **Search** button
2. Click on the name of the Account Record *Pyramid Construction Inc.*
3. Scroll to the Contacts related list and click the **New Contact** button
4. Enter the following information (use the tab key to move from field to field):

   First Name: Gregory

   Last Name: Levitt

   Title: SVP, Administration and Finance

   Department: Finance

   Phone: 505.333.3303

   Email: gregory@pyramid.net
5. Click the **Save** button

Notes

Agenda

- ▶ Welcome & Introductions
- ▶ Setting up a Practice Site
- ▶ Terminology
- ▶ A Tour of Salesforce
- ▶ Leads
- ▶ Activities
- ▶ Converting Leads
- ▶ Accounts
- ▶ Contacts
- ▶ **Opportunities**
- ▶ Reports & Dashboards
- ▶ Putting it All Together
- ▶ Cool Tips!

60

Notes

Updating an Opportunity

John Smith from ABC Labs calls and gives you information regarding his company's time frame to purchase and also mentions that he is ready to receive some preliminary pricing on widgets.

In order for this movement and new information to be reflected in your pipeline, you'll want to move the stage forward and update close date of the Opportunity.

What do you do?

Notes

61

Scenario: Updating an Opportunity

- Search for the Opportunity Record
- Edit the Opportunity
- Save the Record
- Log the call from the Opportunity record

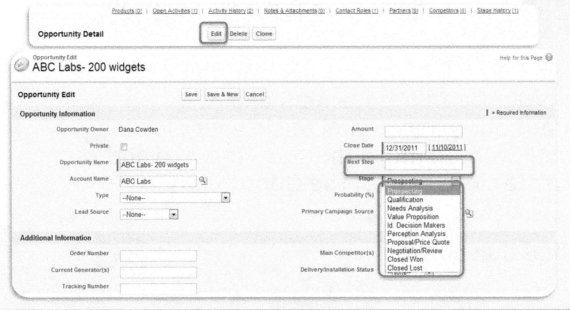

Notes

62

Action Steps: Updating an Opportunity

Goal:

While on the phone with your customer Lauren Wilson, she mentions that Stony International needs to purchase the widgets by no later than the end of next month. She requests that you send her a price quote for the widgets as soon as possible so she can send it to the finance department for approval. You need to update the Amount, Close Date and opportunity Stage to reflect these changes.

Steps:

1. In the global search box, enter the word *Stony* and click the **Search** button
2. Click on the name of the Opportunity Record **Stony International – 200 widgets**
3. Click the **Edit** button on the Opportunity Record
4. Update the following fields based on the information below (use the letter K, M, or B to indicate thousands, millions, or billions in the amount field):

    Amount: 30k

    Close Date: Click in the date field to show the calendar and select the last day of next month

    Stage: Proposal/Price Quote
5. Click the **Save** button

Notes

Agenda

- ▶ Welcome & Introductions
- ▶ Setting up a Practice Site
- ▶ Terminology
- ▶ A Tour of Salesforce
- ▶ Leads
- ▶ Activities
- ▶ Converting Leads
- ▶ Accounts
- ▶ Contacts
- ▶ Opportunities
- ▶ **Reports & Dashboards**
- ▶ Putting it All Together
- ▶ Cool Tips!

Notes

64

Reports Overview

The information you see in reports is data to which you have access. This may include:

- Records you own
- Records you are able to view or edit, but you may not own
- Records that have been shared with you
- Fields that are visible or editable to you

In general, if you can search for and access the records in Salesforce, you will be able to report on them.

Notes

65

Reports - Navigation

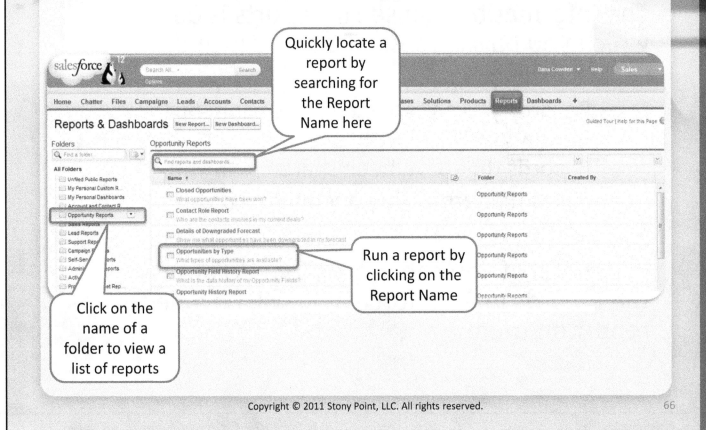

Quickly locate a report by searching for the Report Name here

Run a report by clicking on the Report Name

Click on the name of a folder to view a list of reports

66

Notes

66

Running Reports

STONYPOINT

You have a monthly meeting with your Sales Director to review your pipeline of opportunities set to close within the next 120 days.

In preparation for the meeting, you'd like to review your pipeline.

What should you do?

Notes

67

Scenario: Running Reports

- Select a Report Folder
- Click on the Report Name Link to run it
- Change the Scope information and Re-Run the report

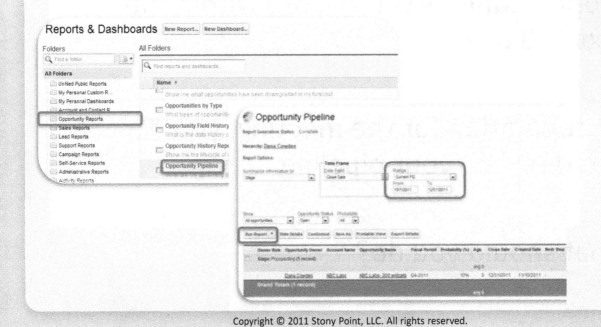

Notes

Action Steps: Running a Report

Goal:

You're having a meeting with your Regional Sales Manager this afternoon regarding opportunities closing in the current calendar year. In preparation for the meeting, you want to run a report of the opportunities in your pipeline for the current CY.

Steps:

1. Click on the **Reports** tab
2. In the folder pane, click on the **Opportunity Reports** folder
3. Scroll through the list of reports and click on the link for the **Opportunity Pipeline** report
4. From the Range pick list menu, select **Current CY**
5. Click the **Run Report** button and review your results

Notes

Dashboard Overview

- A Dashboard is a graphical representation of your data in Salesforce.
  - Comprised of charts, tables, or graphs called components.
- The information you see on a dashboard is data to which you have access.
- To see the most current data, you may need to refresh your Dashboards.
- In most cases, clicking on a Chart will immediately drill through to the customized report behind it.

*Please note that in your Developer Edition for this class, custom reports and dashboards have not been created.

Notes

Dashboards - Navigation

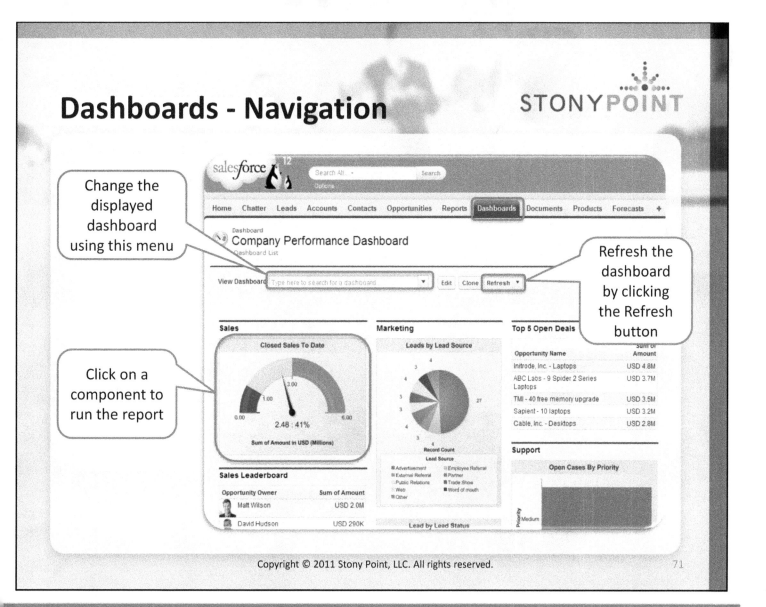

71

Notes

71

Dashboards - Navigation

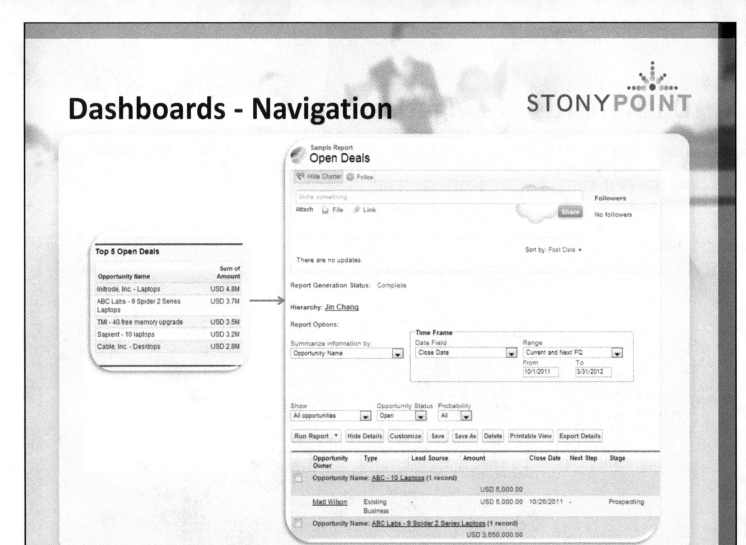

72

Notes

Agenda

▸ Welcome & Introductions
▸ Setting up a Practice Site
▸ Terminology
▸ A Tour of Salesforce
▸ Leads
▸ Activities
▸ Converting Leads
▸ Accounts
▸ Contacts
▸ Opportunities
▸ Reports & Dashboards
▸ **Putting it All Together**
▸ Cool Tips!

Notes

Putting it all Together

Now that you are familiar with the different features of Salesforce, how do you put it all together to work for you?

The following slides are examples of how you can use Salesforce to manage your daily business.

74

Notes

74

Putting it All Together

Goal:

I want to view all of my scheduled calls for the day.

Action:

To view all activities you've created including open and closed tasks and events, use the Activities Tab Plus, installed at the beginning of this course.

*Activities Tab Plus is available at no cost on the Force.com AppExchange. Ask your company's salesforce.com administrator to install it.

75

Notes

Putting it All Together

Goal:

I want to see if I have any new Leads have been assigned to me.

Action:

To view all Leads that have been assigned to you, select the *My Unread Leads* view from the Leads tab.

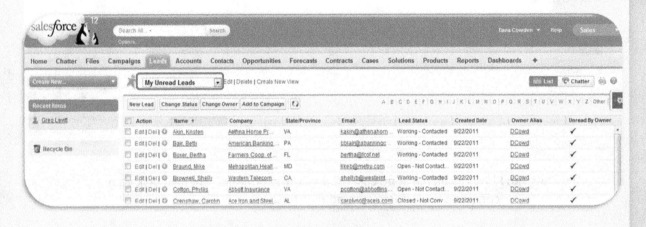

76

Notes

76

Putting it All Together

Goal:

I want to review items in my pipeline.

Action:

To view a list of your opportunities, select the *My Opportunities* view from the Opportunities tab and sort by clicking on the Stage column header.

Notes

Putting it All Together

Goal:

I left a message for a prospect this morning and would like to remind myself to follow up next week.

Action:

From the Lead record, Log a call from the Activity History related list and create a follow up task at the same time.

78

Notes

Putting it All Together

Goal:

Before I visit with one of my Accounts, I'd like to review all of my recent activity with them.

Action:

From the Account record, locate the Activity History related list and review the items.

Notes

79

Agenda

- ▶ Welcome & Introductions
- ▶ Setting up a Practice Site
- ▶ Terminology
- ▶ A Tour of Salesforce
- ▶ Leads
- ▶ Activities
- ▶ Converting Leads
- ▶ Accounts
- ▶ Contacts
- ▶ Opportunities
- ▶ Reports & Dashboards
- ▶ Putting it All Together
- ▶ **Cool Tips!**

80

Notes

80

Tips and Tricks!

- Make login.salesforce.com your "Home Page" for your browser.
  - This will save you time logging into Salesforce when you begin your day

- Open a new window when you are using Salesforce.
  - Hold the "Shift" key while clicking a link with your left mouse button **OR**
  - Right click a link and then select "Open in New Window" from the menu

- Open a new tab when you are using Salesforce
  - Hold the "CTRL" key while clicking a link with your left mouse button **OR**
  - Right click a link and then select "Open in New Tab"

- Use the "Recent Items" list to return to a record that you recently accessed.
  - Located on the left side bar, and is almost always accessible from every record

Notes

Survey

Please take this time to fill out the course survey.

Your instructor will send an email with login instructions.

Notes

82

Question and Answer

STONYPOINT

Please take this time to ask the instructor questions on what you've learned in class.

For additional training, please visit www.stonyp.com.

Notes